Daily Warm-Up Exercises
For Saxophone

by Jackie McLean

cover–drawing by Jackie McLean

computer enhancement by Sharis–Hardkore Enterprise

engraving–Frank Gordon

ISBN 978-0-7935-6365-4

HAL•LEONARD®
CORPORATION
7777 W. BLUEMOUND RD. P.O. BOX 13819 MILWAUKEE, WI 53213

T0019647

"Jackie McLean's enormous contribution to American music makes it imperative for serious players and students to absorb the offerings of this book."

Sonny Rollins
April 15, 1995

"When the name Jackie McLean is read or spoken those informed immediately know that quality, talent and alacrity are evident."
"This master musician/composer/saxophonist has such a wealth of knowledge and experience that we <u>all</u> listen when he speaks – linguistically or musically. The wonderful thing about him is that he continually shares his mind, his heart, his saxophone and his pen."
"Fortunately for us he has taught his saxophone to never speak meaninglessly. The world could use more Jackie McLeans."

Benny Golson
April 14, 1995
New York City

"Jackie McLean is one of the great masters of modern American music. I would highly recommend this book to any musician serious about the art of improvisation."

Branford Marsalis
October 4, 1994

"It would be impossible to transfer his enormous gift by virtue of this book. These insights from the great McLean cannot but help the serious aspiring player. They should be studied."

Sonny Rollins

Preface

The warm-up exercises in this book are designed to help the student become familiar with playing through different keys ascending and descending chromatically. Most books present scales one at a time. Each scale is presented as a singular study. In the beginning this is necessary. One should be thoroughly familiar with each individual key. Once this is accomplished, the exercises in this book will help those that want to improvise. That is why I designed the exercises ascending and descending through the keys. Originally I used these exercises myself as a daily warm-up. One should MEMORIZE these scales and chords just as they are presented in the book. All of my students use this method. Many of them have gone on to be famous like Antoine Roney, Sue Terry, Tom Chapin, Abraham Burton, Tom Murray, Phillip Harper, Steve Davis, Alan Palmer, Eric Mathews, Richard Boulger, Kris Jensen, Greg Banazak, Mary Davis and so many others. My first student was my son Rene McLean. Rene is now teaching at the University of Capetown using this same method with his students there.

I would like to thank two of my former students for helping me with this project. Richard Boulger for encouraging me to create this book, as well as transcribing the solo "Dig," and Eric Matthews for transcribing the solo "Bluesnik", and for synthesizing my method into "The Grand Exercise."

A special thank you to my wife Dollie for all of her support and help with this book.

Jackie McLean

Biography

Jackie McLean was born in New York City in 1932. When he was 12 years old the family moved to the Sugar Hill section of Harlem, a thriving cultural neighborhood where many of the era's foremost writers, artists, actors and musicians lived. The young McLean saw and admired many of them.

His godfather, Norman Cobbs, a saxophonist who played in Adam Clayton Powell's Abyssiania Baptist Church, gave Jackie his first instrument, a soprano saxophone, when he was 14 years old. A year later, he received an alto saxophone from his mother and stepfather. Working in his stepfather's record store, Jackie listened to records of Lester Young and Dexter Gordon. He developed a preference for the harder tenor sound that influenced McLean's unique tone and sound, which is world renown and quite distinct among alto saxophonists.

Within a year Jackie was studying with the pianist Bud Powell and began a very rapid musical development. Thelonious Monk invited McLean to sit in, though the young musician felt that he was not yet ready. It was Charlie Parker, however, who was to have the most profound impact on McLean as a musician, not only verbally encouraging his playing, but even sometimes using the younger musician as a substitute on jobs that Parker himself was unable to fulfill.

By the time he was nineteen years old, though only playing for four years, McLean was already making a name for himself. He had made his recording debut with Miles Davis, and was well on his way to working out an original musical extension of the Parker influence. A period with Charles Mingus, followed by a three-year stint with the drummer, Art Blakey, saw McLean develop as one of the true masters of his instrument. During this time he also began to record under his own name.

In 1959 McLean added acting to his artistic skills, becoming a member of the avant-garde Living Theater. He was cast in Jack Gelber's *The Connection*, performing in both this country and in Europe. He also appeared in the play's film version.

During the 1960's McLean was one of the few established "bebop" players to embrace new developments in music. He introduced many adventurous young stylists to the jazz scene, including Charles Tolliver, Tony Williams, Jack DeJohnette, Larry Willis, and Rene McLean. It was also at this time that he started a Sunday afternoon series in an East Village saloon that eventually became one of the world's most celebrated jazz clubs – Slug's Saloon.

Since 1971, Jackie McLean has lived in Hartford, Connecticut, and added impressive accomplishments to his life's history. Teaching at the Hartt College of Music at the University of Hartford, he developed the jazz degree program and is chairman of the African American Music Department. As a full professor, his course on the history of jazz places the music in its historical, social, and economic context. He also teaches saxophone and improvisation. As a community activist, he, along with his wife, Dollie, spearheaded the establishment of the Artists Collective, Inc., a non-profit multi-arts cultural center. Now in its second decade, the Collective offers training to youth and adults in many art forms, with emphasis on the contributions of African Americans to this nation's arts and culture. A new five million dollar facility for the Artists Collective is in the offing.

Among numerous awards and accolades, Jackie McLean was invited in 1989 to perform in Paris on the occasion of the commemoration of the bicentennial of the French Revolution under the patronage of Danielle Mitterand, wife of the President of France. There he received a medal as *Iffucuer de L'Ordre des Arts des Lettres* from the Minister of Culture, Jack Lang. McLean was honored by New York City's Lincoln Center's Classical Jazz Series with a special evening in concert, "The Music of Jackie McLean" which garnered rave reviews. Jackie McLean continues to perform worldwide with his own group and with other major jazz musicians. Recent recordings on the Triloka label are *Dynasty* and *Rites of Passage* - both featuring his son, multi-instrumentalist, Rene McLean. His most recent recordings on the Polygram label are *Rhythm of the Earth*, *Jackie Mac Attack* and a re-release of *The Complete Blue Note 1964-66 Jackie McLean Sessions* on Mosaic Records. McLean can also be heard on dizzy Gillespie's last recording, *Dizzy Gillespie at the Blue Note*. The McLean's Jazz Dynasty has recently returned from a six-country United States Information Agency - Arts America Tour, which included Namibia, Zimbabwe, Lesotho, Capetown, Johannesburg, and Mozambique. Concerts and special workshops were performed for universities, cultural centers, American Embassies, and many townships, including Soweto.

Jackie McLean was voted number one in the 1993 *Down Beat* Critics Poll and the 1994 *JazzTimes* Readers Poll.

Noted educator, community activist, and celebrated musician, Jackie McLean is proclaimed by peers, critics and audiences as the world premier alto saxophonist of our time.

* Jackie McLean was interviewed by Richard Boulger on October 17, 1994. The interview went as follows. *

Interview

Question: You've played the saxophone for almost fifty years. Having played with many of the masters, what advice on practicing would you share with aspiring saxophonists?

Answer: I would advise that they do a serious daily warm-up that should take at least forty-five minutes. My book requires long tones, scales, and chords. These warm-ups are essential in getting your practice started.

Question: Who were your biggest influences and in what order were you introduced to them?

Answer: My biggest influences were first Lester Young, Dexter Gordon and Charlie Parker.

Question: How can one develop as an improviser?

Answer: By practicing an awful lot and by playing other instruments like the piano, and trying to play different forms like the blues, standards, and modern compositions, as well.

Question: Is there a certain recording that you've made that you're especially proud of?

Answer: I am proud of all of my recordings. I'm always looking forward to the next one. There are many. I think I like *The Connection, Let Freedom Ring,* and the title track on *Monuments.*

Question: What is your concept to improvisation in music?

Answer: My concept is to first know how to play across the instrument through all the keys; develop a good ear; and be able to sing what you want to play. In other words, if you are trying to take someone's solo off of a recording, the first thing you should do is to listen to it enough until it becomes familiar. Then try to sing it, and then try to take it off on the instrument. Always start with something very simple.

Question: Miles Davis has been credited with composing "Dig" even though most people know you were the composer. How did that come about?

Answer: Because it was Miles' record date the producers gave him credit as composer of all the compositions, including my work, "Dig," as well as Sonny Rollins' "Out Of The Blue."

Question: What do you remember about your first record date?

Answer: Many of my biggest influences were in the studio that day. Art Blakey, Sonny Rollins, Miles, and Charles Mingus. Charlie Parker was there the whole record date. That was very frightening, although he was the one who made me feel comfortable. He told me to relax and that I sounded good.

Table of Contents

Long Tone Warm - Up Exercise

Attack each note without tonguing (even the low notes).   Play each note below five times:
1.) Loud 2.) Medium 3.) Soft 4.) Medium 5.) Loud.   Hold each note as long as you can.

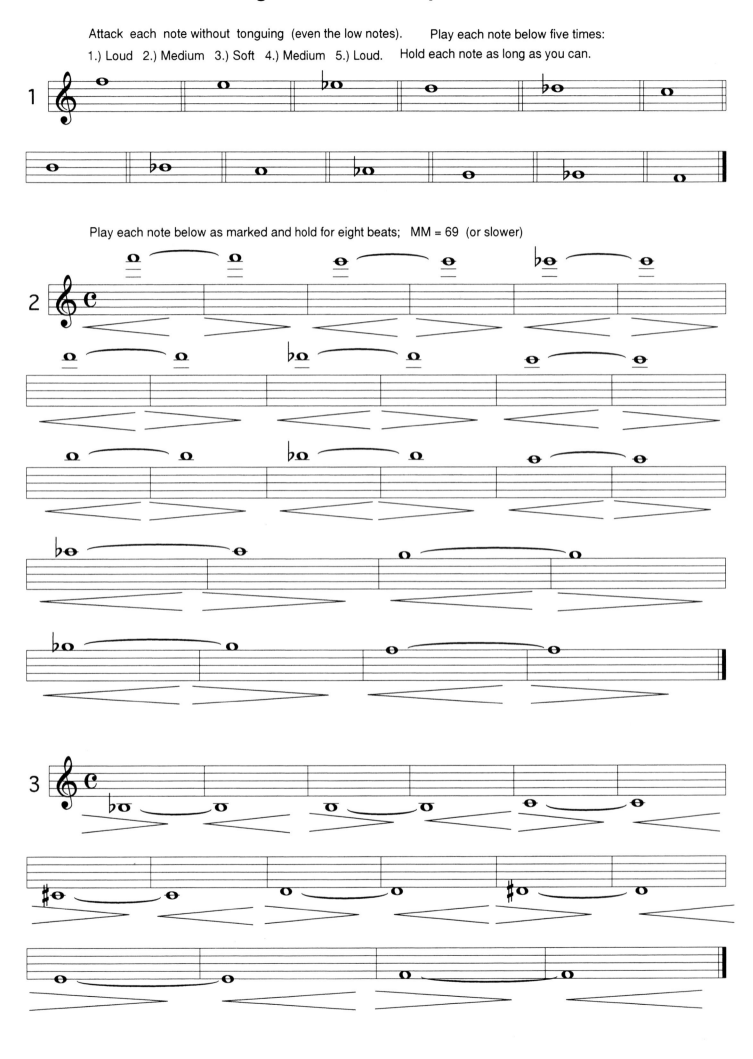

Play each note below as marked and hold for eight beats;   MM = 69 (or slower)

MAJOR CHORDS

MINOR CHORDS

11

AUGMENTED CHORDS

12

13

DIMINISHED CHORDS

14

GRAND EXERCISE

Augmented

16

Major

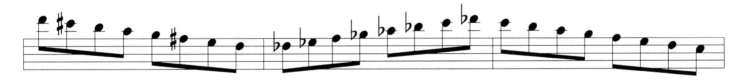

Minor

Diminished

Minor

23

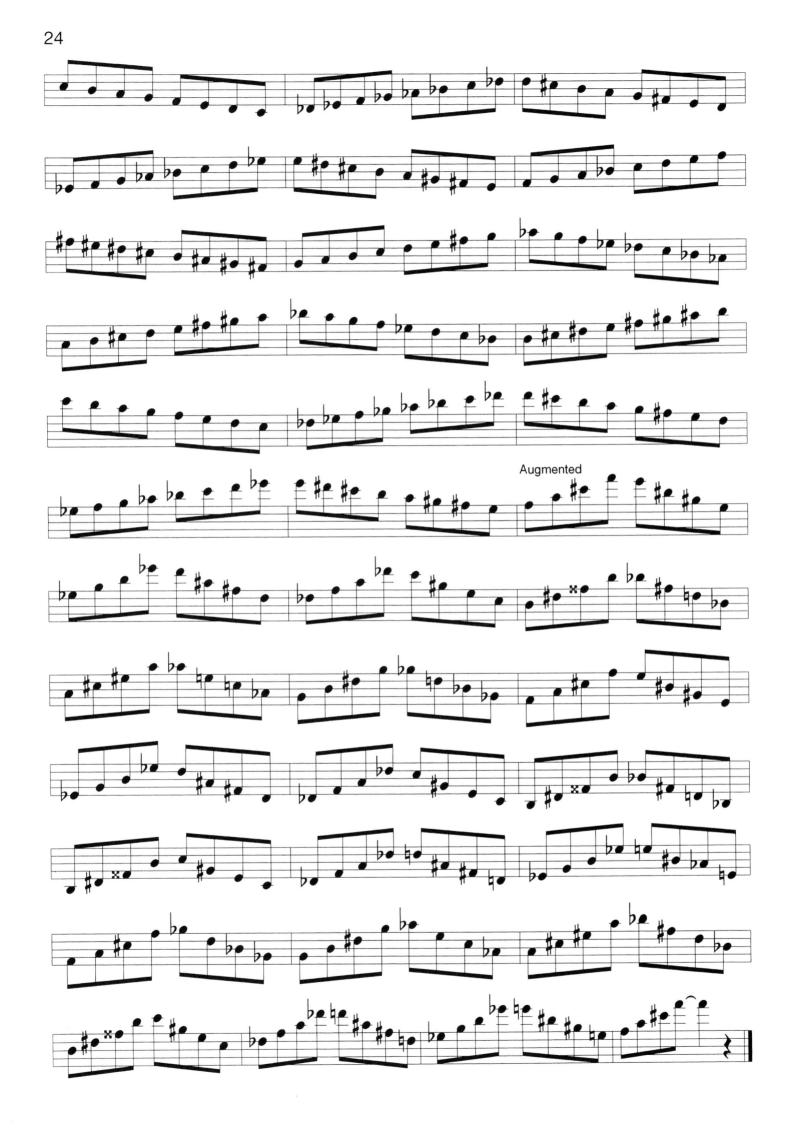

Augmented

BLUESNIK

Solo by Jackie McLean
Transcribed by Eric Matthews

Composition by Jackie McLean
Recorded on BLUESNIK
Blue Note BST-84067

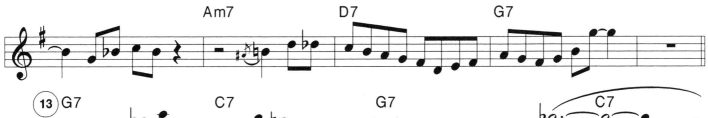

DIG

Solo by Jackie McLean
Transcribed by Richard Boulger

Composition by Jackie McLean
Recorded on DIG - Miles Davis
Prestige Lp 7012

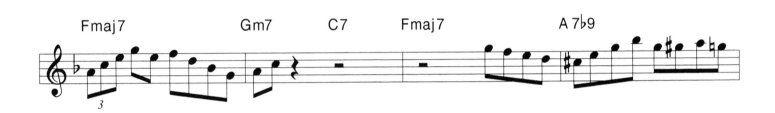